# MORE THAN
# MY JOB'S WORTH

# MORE THAN MY JOB'S WORTH

Howard Lester

CONSTABLE

Constable & Robinson Ltd
55-56 Russell Square
London WC1B 4HP
This edition published by Constable,
an imprint of Constable & Robinson Ltd 2012

A copy of the British Library Cataloguing in Publication Data
is available from the British Library

ISBN-13: 978-1-47210-254-6
Designed by Design 23
Printed and bound in the European Union


1 3 5 7 9 10 8 6 4 2

# Contents

# Introduction

Why is it that some people, given a little bit of authority, feel the urge to use it to thwart and frustrate their fellow citizens? Modern life seems to be full of jobsworth joylessness. From the council workers who invent absurd rules and regulations to the health and safety zealots who would ban fun if they could, and from the ticket inspectors who delight in finding minor problems to the parking attendants whose only pleasure is catching a hapless driver a few inches over the yellow line: there is an army of people out to interfere and obstruct you as you attempt to pass through your daily life in peace. This book collects some of the most absurd examples of jobsworthery. Be warned: these anecdotes might amuse or enrage you, depending on how recently you have been the victim of your own local jobsworths.

—◠◠—

# Tickets Please

*The phrase 'more than my job's worth' was originally the catchphrase of those surly ticket inspectors who made travelling on the old British Rail trains such a joy. In general, the role of checking tickets seems to lead inexorably towards pointless obstruction and petty interference in one's existence…*

—◠◠—

## No Good Samaritans

When comedian Tom Wrigglesworth tried to help a fellow passenger, he didn't expect to be threatened with arrest as a result. He was on a train from Manchester to Euston when he witnessed an elderly lady being badgered by the ticket inspector. Her £11.50 ticket had a misprint and didn't match her travel confirmation documents – one said she was on the 10.45 train, the other said the 10.15. Station staff advised her to get the earlier train.

However the ticket inspector wouldn't accept her explanation and insisted she pay the £115 full fare because her ticket wasn't valid. Mr Wrigglesworth could see the distress this was causing her, so he decided that the best way to help was to organise a whip-round among his fellow passengers. They had all seen the inspector's bullying behaviour and several of them were happy to help out.

At this point the frustrated ticket collector called

British transport police and reported Mr Wrigglesworth for 'begging on the train'. He was met at Euston and interrogated by two officers. He was lucky to escape arrest, as some of his fellow passenters saw what was happening and intervened to vouch for his behaviour.

## Back Home

Three soldiers on leave from Afghanistan were threatened with arrest and instructed to get off a train by the ticket inspector. They were on their way home from Helmand province for two weeks leave when they were told that their rail warrants couldn't be accepted .

Their flight had been due to land at RAF Brize Norton in Oxfordshire, so they had warrants to change at Oxford. However they actually landed at East Midlands Airport after the plane ran into bad weather. The three soldiers, who were dressed in combats and had their kit bags, got a train from East Midlands Parkway station. Their fatal mistake was to assume that any reasonable ticket inspector would understand how the diversion had affected their plans.

## The Olympic Spirit

Former government minister David Blunkett reacted with shock and anger when an officious ticket collector prevented him from taking his seat at the 2012 Paralympics opening ceremony in London. Mr Blunkett, who has been blind since birth, was told he couldn't take his allotted seat because he had his guide dog with him.

The official, described by the MP as being 'stroppy and insensitive', blocked the way, and after Mr Blunkett asked him to show some common sense, eventually backed down, but only to the extent that a seat was found elsewhere on an 'exposed, blustery gantry', from which Mr Blunkett had to watch the show for the next three-and-a-half hours.

—ɯɯ—

# Health and Safety

*We could fill an entire book with examples of 'health and safety gone mad'. While some sensible decisions are made to protect the public, there is always that one official or department who decide that the only way they can keep us safe is to wrap us in cotton wool and remove all sharp objects within a three mile radius. Here are a few of the more ridiculous examples.*

—ɯɯ—

## Engineering Hanging Baskets

Villagers in Coton-in-the-Elms in Derbyshire were amazed to discover that they needed to pay for a structural engineer if they wanted to hang flower baskets on lamp posts. The villagers, who wanted to brighten up the area, asked their local council if they could put flowering baskets on the lamp posts and were told that each one would need to be assessed by a structural engineer at a cost of £70 per post, which would have resulted in a bill of over £1,000. The reason? The council's deeply neurotic health and safety department were afraid that the flowering baskets might fall on someone's head and cause an injury.

Resident David Brookes said: 'When was the last time someone got injured by a hanging basket? We're a voluntary organisation just trying to do our best to make the village look nice and tidy for the summer, and the council have stopped us. It's petty and bureaucratic.'[1]

1 *The Sun* 7th June 2012

Perhaps he should have remember that some councils regard 'petty' and 'bureaucratic' as the highest compliments possible.

## Acceptable Gnomes

Council chiefs in Tipton in the West Midlands were forced into an embarrassing U-turn after they had banned garden gnomes on health and safety grounds.

Linda Langford, 57, was informed that two garden gnomes outside her council flat were a fire hazard and could be tripped over. She said: 'It's barmy. The idea my gnomes are dangerous in any way is ridiculous.'[2]

The councillor concerned had originally said: 'This is about fire regulations. Whatever people say, safety comes first.' However, he eventually apologised and accepted that the rules had been misinterpreted. He said: 'As long as there is not an excessive number of gnomes, or similar items, they can stay.' Ms Langford

2 *Daily Mirror*, 1st Dec 2009

was also told that she could keep her doormat and welcome plaque, which had also been included in the original ban.

## Hot Hot Hot

A café in Devon refused to give a mother a mug of hot water so that she could put a jar of baby food in it to warm up. They said that there was a risk of the baby being scalded and therefore health and safety rules would not allow it. At the time the mother was drinking a hot cup of tea.

## Scaffolding is Banned

One North London council recently informed residents that the major works due to be carried out on their homes would not include any work on the roof or guttering. The reason given was that they were carrying out a health and safety review on their scaffolding policy and until this was complete their staff were not allowed to use scaffolding at all. When questioned, they were unable to say when the review would be completed.

## Blu-tack Peril

A school in Perth and Kinross in Perthshire banned teachers from using the adhesive gum blu-tack on its windows because the health and safety department told them it would make the glass in the windows explode. Officials, clearly on a mission to prevent anyone being subjected to the sight of children's artwork, decided that blu-tack would react with a chemical in the glass that would cause it to shatter.

They duly ordered that all art should be removed from the windows. The school, which is run by a private company, had no choice but to comply. Teachers pointed out that it actually states on the packet that blu-tack can be used on glass, but to no avail. The company that runs the school declined to comment.

## Too Hot

One hospital banned a visitor from heating a patient's meal in a microwave on the grounds of health and safety, even though they served hot food at mealtimes themselves.

## Unknown Danger

Walsall Council put up a new sign on Broadway Playing Fields banning all ball games on its playing fields because of health and safety rulings. Although the playing fields have been in use for many years the council now say that part of them may be over a landfill site that could be problematic although they admit not knowing what the land is actually 'filled' with.

The council refused to explain exactly what the health and safety concerns were or what dangers ball games posed compared to other traditional games such as 'hide and seek', 'sprint races' or 'tag'.

## Danger in the Garden

A care home in Southampton was ordered to remove all its garden decorations within 28 days on health and safety grounds. They were sent a list of items that had to be removed. Roses were not allowed to be grown on account of the fact that rose thorns may cause 'cuts and abrasions'. Garden furniture such as chairs and benches presented a 'trip hazard' to residents and pot plants were deemed 'an obstruction to ground maintenance teams'. Even the birds weren't excused: the bird table was listed as 'restricting access to the windows'.

The housing association that owns the home

threatened to destroy all offending items and send them the bill if the residents refused to comply. All complaints fell upon deaf ears. The housing association insisted that the home already had small areas for planting flowers and it was in the terms of the lease that these must not be extended.

## Milk Crate Panic

For fifteen years, children at Wychwood Primary School in Oxfordshire had happily played with plastic milk crates donated by a local dairy company. However, the local authority removed the milk crates without warning, and made the dairy company take them back, telling the school that they might injure children who played with them. No child had ever actually been injured in this way but the local council insisted that you can't be too careful. They cited new health and safety rules as the reason for their prompt action. The school called the decision 'outrageous.'

## No Swinging

Fun-loving health and safety officials in South Yorkshire ordered a mother to remove her children's swing from her allotment or face it being forcibly removed and destroyed. Apparently, it is fine to put a child's swing in a privately owned garden not on land rented from the council. On rented land, swings are a health and safety risk because they may lead to injury.

What happens to tenants in council houses who put play equipment in their gardens? The local council refused to comment on this conundrum.

## Irons are Dangerous

West Sussex County Council removed all ironing boards from the Caravan Club caravan site in East Grinstead. Council officials (presumably wearing crumpled clothing) claimed that anyone who used the ironing boards could get burned.

Members of the Caravan Club were stunned at the decision but the ironing boards were never returned. A council spokesperson said 'It is a legal requirement to ensure that electrical equipment is maintained in a safe condition' but later admitted that 'the type and frequency of testing is up to its owners.'

Anyone wanting to stay at the campsite is advised to bring non-iron clothing.

## The Wrong Trainers

A man visiting a London gym was told he couldn't lift weights because he wasn't wearing the right sort of trainers.

## No Tea At The Fete

A parent teacher association at a school in Uxbridge, Middlesex was warned that serving tea at the school's summer fete was too dangerous. Council killjoys said: 'A risk assessment for running a school fete will be appropriate. It is not about creating huge amounts of paperwork, but rather about identifying sensible and proportionate measures to protect helpers and young children from risks that cause real harm.'[3]

When asked whether or not the school could serve coffee instead, they refused to answer.


## No Candles

Police stormed a three-year-old's birthday party to prevent his mum from lighting the candles on his cake. Police officers were called to Oscar Barlow's third birthday party at Rumble Tumble play centre in Hanley, Stoke-on-Trent, because his parents lit the candles in violation of heath and safety regulations.

The owners of the Rumble Tumble play centre claimed that candles presented a health and safety risk and said Oscar's mum, Natasha Bent, could light the candles, but only in a special supervised area,

3 *The Sun* June 2012

overseen by members of staff. After discussing this with the staff, and becoming increasingly frustrated with their approach, Natasha took the cake to the car park to light it, at which point the police were called. Oscar was left in tears as two police officers accused his mum of behaving in an intimidating manner.

Ms Bent said: 'When we were there we brought in Oscar's birthday cake from the car, but just as we were going to light the candles they told us we couldn't. All we wanted to do was sing Happy Birthday and have Oscar blow out the candles… How on earth would a child get injured by singing Happy Birthday? It was a bad way for a three-year-old to experience a birthday. It's a special occasion and his first one understanding what a birthday is.'[4]

The fun-loving owners of Rumble Tumble declined to comment on their deep seated fear of birthday cakes.

---

4 *The Daily Mail* 14th May 2012

## Flip Flop Flap

A woman was banned by her boss from wearing flip flop sandals to the office. He told her that they were a health and safety hazard because she could easily trip over in them. She was ordered to wear footwear with a 'supported toe and enclosed back'.

## Potty Potholes

When one South Manchester resident asked the council to fill in a pothole that was creating problems in his road, he was told that his request would be referred to the 'pothole scrutiny committee'.

## No Children

A nursery worker was banned by her local council from taking children to her allotment. The woman had wanted to help the little children to grow cress in jars so that they could learn about growing. However, the council's health and safety department told her that she was not to allow the children onto her allotment because other allotment users had complained it was 'inappropriate' for children to be there. Apparently, complaints had been made about the fencing on the allotment, which was meant to safeguard the children.

## Rained Off

A school sports day was cancelled due to wet weather and wet conditions on the school field. The reason given was health and safety.

## No Sunglasses

A man had been advised by his doctor to wear sunglasses at work due to light related headaches. He worked in an office with a glass roof and on sunny days found the light made him very uncomfortable. His boss, however, refused to allow it on health and safety grounds. He was not even allowed to wear glasses that reacted to light and became sunglasses in bright weather.

## Doormat Danger

A housing association ordered the removal of all doormats in resident's homes as they presented a slipping and tripping health and safety issue.

## Mossy Challenge

The Royal Mail refused to deliver post to a business in Leicestershire after a postman fell and broke his shoulder in bad weather. The postman had slipped on moss on the pavement in cold damp weather conditions.

## Danger Everywhere

A housing association told residents in a block of flats that all their letter boxes had to be sealed up for health and safety reasons in case the block was firebombed. Notice boards in the entrance were also removed in case they came loose, fell off the wall and hit someone walking past.

## Parking Deception

A Royal Mail Depot in the East Midlands put up a sign telling customers that they could no longer use the car park due to 'health and safety' rules. After receiving a deluge of complaints the depot finally admitted that they had only put up the signs so that the car park could be left for staff only to use.

## The Cycle of Life

A college that was promoting walking and cycling to its campus refused requests for a bicycle lending scheme in case they were prosecuted in the event of an accident. People could borrow bicycles elsewhere as long as they didn't fall off in the college grounds.

## Cone Alert

A woman asked her local council to provide her with some cones in the street to reserve space for the removal van on the day she moved house. The council refused on the grounds of health and safety in case drivers didn't notice them and crashed.

## Lengthy Swim

A parent was prevented by a pool lifeguard from taking their eight-year-old into the deep end at a swimming pool. The child was a strong swimmer who could swim two lengths of the pool and his father was accompanying him so he was perfectly safe. However, the lifeguard told his father that children had to be able to swim three lengths of the pool before being allowed in the deep end.

## Food Safety

A historical re-enactment society was told that they could not use vegetables to simulate beheadings and stabbings because the rules on chopping vegetables in a public place were not being followed. Only one person could 'chop' while the rest had to watch from a few metres away.

## Ladder Madness

GCSE students putting on a school performance as part of their course were told by their local authority that the production could not go ahead because the boy operating the stage lights had not been on a 'fixed ladder training course'.

## No Sharpeners

A 14-year-old girl was banned from buying a pencil sharpener because it was allegedly too dangerous. A cashier at the high-street store had been told that only people aged eighteen and over could buy them.

Emily Davies from Poole, Dorset, tried to buy a stationery set containing the sharpener but said: 'The woman asked to see my ID because she said the set contained 'lethal objects'. I was puzzled and she said 'It has a pencil sharpener, it could be dangerous.' But I've bought stuff like that before for school and it was fine. I can't really imagine someone over 18 wanting

something like a school stationery set. It was all a bit unnecessary.'[5]

Eventually Emily went back to the shop with her eighteen-year-old brother and got him to buy it after showing his driving license as ID. He then handed it to Emily in front of the cashier and she put it into her bag. Their mother Susan Davies said: 'It seemed so ridiculous. I didn't really believe the children when they told me what had happened. What's it going to be next? Pupils having to have their pencils sharpened for them at school? I can't work out what damage you can do with a pencil sharpener.'

A spokesperson said it the shop had no firm age policy on buying pencil sharpeners but that they would rather their staff be over-cautious on such matters and defended the zealous cashier's refusal to allow school girls to sharpen their pencils.

---

5 *The Daily Mail* 21st March 2012

## Get That Gull

When a seagull became caught up in a plastic bag at Carshalton Ponds in Sutton, Surrey, 25 fire-fighters were called out to rescue it. However, the local council's health and safety rules meant that they were banned from wading into the 3ft deep pond. The fire crews then stood by and watched as 20-year-old Adam Briddock, an animal rescue volunteer from the Riverside Animal Centre, waded into the water to help the bird instead. The rescued bird was taken to the centre where it was allowed to dry out, fed, and released back into the wild the next day.

The founder of the Riverside Centre, Ted Burden, said: 'It was a bit ridiculous really. Five fire crews turned up, but because of protocols they could not go into the water. It is health and safety gone mad really, when you look at it, because the water was not really any more than waist deep.'

A spokesperson for the London Fire Brigade

insisted that avoiding any danger was vital for fire-fighters. He said: 'It was a standard response to an animal being in trouble, and the fire fighters were on hand in case a member of public had tried to rescue the bird or the water rescue team had got into trouble. We are not willing to put the lives of our fire-fighters at risk for the sake of a seagull. Our fire-fighters get called out to lots of different incidents and never know what they are going to find when they get there.'[6]

---

6 *The Daily Mail* 12th Apr 2012

—∿—

# The Joy of Parking

*Who hasn't had the infuriating experience of searching in vain for a spot where you are allowed to park or even pause in your car? Luckily there are usually helpful wardens on hand, pens permanently poised, ready to issue a ticket if any mishap or accident should cause you to momentarily transgress their baffling rules…*

—∿—

## You're Just Doing Your Job, We're Just Doing Ours…

Westminster Council in London zealously enforce their parking regulations. In January 2006, an 18ft (5m) northern bottle-nosed whale tragically found itself stranded in the River Thames. As the British Divers Marine Life Rescue team struggled to save the whale's life, traffic wardens gave their vehicles parking tickets. Police had given them permission to park by the river, but the traffic wardens said they had not been made aware that parking permission had been given. They subsequently insisted that it was in any case Westminster Council who decided who could park where – not the police.

## The Wrong Ticket

A shopper in Marlow was left with a hefty parking fine after visiting a new branch of Sainsbury's. The man parked in the supermarket's new car park and bought a ticket at the 'Pay and Display' machine. He then displayed the ticket on the dashboard and went inside the shop. However, it turned out that what he believed to be a parking ticket was in fact a voucher for the store. The new parking machines were handing out receipts, tickets and store vouchers whenever someone bought a parking ticket. Others were also left confused by the system. Although the store eventually changed the machines to give out the parking ticket, receipt

and voucher in one strip, it was less sympathetic to the earlier customers who had been mistaken about the ticket they put in their car windows. The local council insisted on upholding their fines because posters were displayed explaining the system to motorists and said motorists should 'check that they have put the correct ticket on their dashboard'.

## No Excuses

In London in 2011, motorcycle courier Carl Brownsman was hit by a car as he rode his motorbike down a busy London street. The bike was a complete write-off and he needed to be taken to hospital immediately. As paramedics carefully lifted him into the back of the ambulance, a traffic warden appeared and insisted on giving the man a parking ticket for leaving his motorbike by the curb. The motorbike in question was a total wreck after the collision and paramedics explained the urgency of the situation but the traffic warden refused to listen, pointing out that the bike was in a 'no parking' zone and therefore liable for a fine even though it could only have been moved by a rescue vehicle.

## A Helping Hand

In Nottingham in 2010, Mr Sadiq stopped his mini cab by the curb to help a passenger in the back seat who had become suddenly ill. As Mr Sadiq telephoned for an ambulance, standing by his car to get better reception on his mobile phone, a traffic warden helpfully issued him with a parking ticket. Mr Sadiq explained the situation to the warden who replied that it was not his business to consider whether someone was ill or not, he was only concerned with patrolling double yellow lines. Insane job done, he then wandered off without giving the ill passenger as much as a backward glance. It can only be hoped that he never finds himself in need of a good Samaritan…

## No Stopping

Sam Fenton, a long-distance lorry driver, was driving his eighteen-wheeler down a busy road in Cardiff when the road beneath the lorry partially collapsed leaving him unable to continue because some of the wheels became trapped in the recently appeared holes. Flash floods had weakened the road surface and the road had simply caved in. Mr Fenton telephoned for assistance and a tow truck was sent out. However, while he was waiting for it to arrive, a traffic warden issued him with a parking ticket for being in a 'no stopping or loading' area. Fenton pointed out that his vehicle was stuck and couldn't possibly be moved but the officious warden insisted that he was 'illegally parked' as there was 'no stopping' along that road

## Must Try Harder

A student received a parking fine even though the ticket machine was out of order. She had left a note on the dashboard explaining that the meter was broken and added her mobile telephone number. Traffic wardens still gave her a fine and it was upheld because it was felt that she could have roamed around the neighbouring streets until she found another parking meter that worked.

## Painted into a Corner

A woman in the Midlands was given a ticket for parking in a disabled bay, that didn't even exist when she parked her car. The next day the woman telephoned her local council to complain and asked them when the parking bay had come into existence. A council employee told her that the bay had been painted the day before. She protested that when she had parked her car it hadn't been in a disabled bay, but the employee insisted that there was nothing they could do. The woman pointed out that whoever painted around her car should have just noted down the registration and waived the fine because when she parked her car it had been perfectly legal. The council remained adamant that there was nothing they could do once the fine went 'into the system'.

## Towed Away

A disabled driver had his car towed away from the designated disabled parking space outside their home. On hearing a commotion outside his home the disabled man looked through his window to see the tow truck lifting his car. When he got outside he told the driver that the car was his and that he was disabled. In fact, the parking bay had been put there for him after much pleading with the local council.

The tow truck driver simply told the man that because he couldn't see a blue badge he had no choice but to remove the car. The badge had actually slipped onto the floor but even though the disabled man pointed out that he could simply open the car

door to find the badge the tow truck driver cheerfully told him that the car couldn't be removed from the truck once it had been put there, and drove off.

## 'None of My Business'

A disabled man suffering from motor neurone disease was issued with a parking ticket as he helped his elderly mother-in-law into a hospital in Leicestershire.It was raining heavily when David Ellis, who had suffered from the muscle wasting disease for four years, arrived at his local hospital only to discover that all the disabled parking bays were full. Due to his disability, he parked his car in the closest available pay-and-display parking bay with his blue disabled parking badge clearly on view inside the front windscreen.

As he struggled to help the 86-year-old lady into her wheelchair, a parking attendant appeared and began calmly writing out a ticket for his car. Mr Ellis tried to explain the situation but the warden's response was that it was 'none of my business.' After handing over the ticket, he started to walk away. Mr Ellis asked for help, but says that 'he belligerently refused and stood by my car with his back to me while I struggled.'

The hospital subsequently apologised for the ticket. Mr Ellis said that although the parking ticket was bad enough he felt stunned by the attendant's attitude and refusal to help. The parking attendant insisted that he was only employed to hand out parking fines and showed no interest in going beyond his remit and coming to the aid of someone who clearly needed help. An equally dismissive spokesperson pointed out that parking attendants were not obliged or insured to help 'in medical emergencies' and that he had therefore acted appropriately.

## Beyond the Grave

In December 2010 an over-zealous traffic warden slapped a parking ticket on a car because it had been parked in a space for too long. The traffic warden failed to notice that the man in the passenger seat was dead.

Police believe that the man suffered a heart attack after returning to his car from a Christmas shopping trip. Another shopper called police after seeing the man slumped at the wheel of his silver Audi. Police confirmed that the man, believed to be in his fifties, was confirmed dead at the scene. Forensic officers recorded the death as not being suspicious.

When the warden who issued the fine was told of the death, he told police that it wasn't his job to peer into cars to see if any passengers needed help. He said: 'My job is to look in the car to see if there is a ticket displayed and how long that ticket is for.'

## Don't Blink...

In Salford in 2009, a traffic warden gave a man a parking ticket for shutting his eyes for five minutes. The warden claimed that she watched him for five minutes before slapping the ticket on his windscreen. She said that local council rules stated that she wasn't allowed to wake someone sleeping in their car in case it frightened them into a heart attack. She also said that in any case she didn't consider it her job to deal with drivers – just their cars and where they were parked.

The driver, who had just driven two hundred miles, claims he just shut his eyes for five minutes because he felt tired, and then woke to find himself being issued a parking ticket. The traffic warden ran off before he was able to speak to her.

Salford Council soberly issued the following statement: 'The attendant was very apologetic, but said that as she had already started to write out the ticket she couldn't stop. At the time, a man was sleeping in the car but this does not mean that he is exempt from getting a parking ticket. It is not the role of a traffic enforcement officer to wake people up if they are sleeping in their car and the individual concerned should have bought his parking ticket before taking a nap.' They also confirmed that it was against their rules for traffic wardens to touch a vehicle, except for placing parking fines on the windscreen.

## Ignorance Is No Excuse

In January 2004, a woman took her elderly aunt out to dinner and parked her car on a quiet side street. One half of the street had 'No Parking' signs but the other half appeared to have no restrictions. There was a sign but the writing on it had been scratched out and was therefore unreadable. The woman's aunt had a blue disability badge and she displayed this clearly in the front window of the car before heading to the restaurant.

When the two women returned to the car having finished their dinner, the car had a parking ticket on it. The owner of the car appealed to the council, including a photograph of the scratched-out unreadable sign. She was told that 'lack of signage is no excuse for not knowing the rules.'

## Blood Money

In Derby in 2008, traffic wardens issued two mobile blood donor vans with parking tickets because they were parked in a restricted parking area. At the time both vans were in the process of receiving blood from volunteers.

When the medical staff showed the wardens that they had written permission to be parked there, the traffic wardens simply smiled and shrugged. They explained that because the parking permission was given by a different council department to the one they worked for, they were not obliged to pay any attention to it.

## Race You To The Car

A disabled lady from North London, who walks with a stick, parked her car in the West End of London. She wasn't sure whether her Camden disabled parking badge was valid in that area, so she went to look for a traffic warden to ask them. When she finally found a warden she told them where she had parked and was told that no, she wasn't allowed to park there.

The over-excited traffic warden then ran at full speed back to the car in order to be able to issue the lady with a ticket before she had struggled back to her vehicle with her walking stick.

## Making It Up As We Go Along

A man in West Ealing in London agreed to move his car down the road so that workmen who were painting double yellow lines on the road could continue with their job. As soon as the man left his vehicle in the position they had suggested, a traffic warden slapped a parking fine on it. He explained that the whole road was being painted with double yellow lines and the spot where the car was now parked was included. The driver's protestations that he had simply done what he was told and was willing to park anywhere that the warden and workmen agreed to allow him to were sadly to no avail.

## Yellow Line Ambush

Another Londoner driver left for work on the tube one morning with his car legally parked outside his house. When he returned that evening, a yellow line had been painted down the road stopping at his car and then continuing from his car down the road.

A sign saying 'Resident Parking Only' had also appeared. A traffic warden had put a parking fine on his car because he didn't have a residents parking permit. When he telephoned the council to point out that they hadn't been issued with resident parking permits yet, the council said that there was nothing they could do because once the signs had gone up they had to be obeyed.

## £50 For a Nap

A lady pulled off the motorway at around midnight feeling very tired. She was driving home from London to Preston and had been driving in the dark for a couple of hours. She stretched and relaxed on the back seat of her car and, without intending to, fell asleep. When she woke up it was 4:30am and, after getting herself a coffee from the service station, she set off on the rest of her journey home.

A few days later she received a £50 fine in the post. The woman hadn't seen any signs about parking limitations and was shocked. The service station in question admitted that there was no sign regarding a two-hour parking limit but said that they did provide a 'long stay' car park for anyone wishing to spend longer at their services. The woman asked how motorists could possibly know the difference given that there was no sign advising of the hours regarding short and long stay car parks?

The service station reiterated their argument that a four hour stay was not a 'short stay' and upheld the fine. Presumably they weren't satisfied with their profit from the reasonably-priced food and drink on offer…

## Dead Badger, White Stripes

Near the village of Downton on the border of Hampshire and Wiltshire, workmen who were painting white lines along the side of the road painted over a dead badger that had been left by the kerb. Their reason for doing this? Apparently, it was 'not their responsibility' to move a dead animal.

A spokesperson for Hampshire County Council said that the workers did what they thought was the best thing to do since it is not the local council's job to move carcasses from the roads. After much argument, the dead animal was eventually moved and the white lines re-painted. The council refused to comment on whether or not the dead badger had at last received a dignified burial.

## Redefining 'Common Sense'

Residents of Highbury Crescent in North London have often wondered why there is an eighteen-inch-long single yellow line on their street, barely long enough to fit a single tyre, let alone a vehicle. Islington Council insist that it is there to 'help drivers' because it signals a tiny space between two resident parking bays. A councillor from Islington Council said: 'In Islington we take a common sense approach to parking enforcement. This means making sure signs and lines clearly identify the different parking bays we provide for residents and visitors.'[7] It would probably be less confusing for drivers to extend each of the neighbouring parking bays by nine inches and join them together. However this

7 BBC News Sunday, 15th April 2007

would have been against the rules because of the 'maximum width' that parking bays are allowed to be. Who made up this particular rule? Surely it wasn't Islington Council themselves?

It truly is hard to beat a 'common sense approach'.

## No Parking … Anything

A traffic warden slapped a £60 fine on a lifeboat. The vessel in question was in the process of being decommissioned and the crew had left it for a couple of minutes to deal with the necessary paperwork. When they returned to the boat they found a parking fine stuck to the lifeboat covers. The crew were bewildered: the boat was due for retirement and had simply been left on a trailer in a car park as they collected the documents they needed. The eager traffic warden, in Appledore, Devon, jumped at the chance to give the vehicle a parking fine because it did not have a Pay-and-Display parking ticket.

The irony was that the lifeboat was council-owned and the fine meant that the money-hungry council were fining themselves. Niki Tait, from the Royal National Lifeboat Institution (RNLI), said: 'With everything the crew had to do it slipped their minds to even think of getting a parking ticket. It was Torridge District Council's parting donation to the

RNLI. We like most donations, however big or small, but that one we thought was a little unnecessary.'[8]

Following tense negotiations, Torridge District Council cancelled the ticket. This meant they deleted both a credit and a debit of £60 from their books and thus ended up losing nothing but a little shred of their dignity.

8 *Daily Mail* 18th July 2012

—∿—

# The Infinite Wisdom
# of Councils

*Aren't councils brilliant? Such a fine example of local
democracy in action. The community comes together
and elects wise leaders who make sensible decisions
about how the neighbourhood should be run. And
everything runs smoothly thereafter.
Except in the real world, that is very rarely
how things turn out...*

—∿—

**Blowing in the Wind**

In 2006, a Devon woman was accused by the local council of littering when she swept leaves from a tree into the gutter. She and her husband had been clearing leaves from their drive and the pavement for over twelve years. The tree in question belonged to the council as it was planted on the pavement.

However the 61-year-old woman was flabbergasted when a road sweeper told her that she was breaking the law and she was issued with a fine.

Her husband said: 'The tree was pruned five or six years ago and now it's massive. At this time of year our driveway gets covered in its leaves. For years we have been brushing them out in the gutter for the council to pick up. My wife heard the council worker coming down the road in a [motorised] litter cleaner and so she brushed the leaves into a pile in the gutter. The man told her he could not take them away and that she was littering – she was in tears. I heard it going on and went out and he told me we were fly-tipping and he wasn't going to pick up the leaves. I told him they weren't our leaves – they came from the council's tree …They drove off without cleaning up [any of] the leaves.' [9]

Torbay Council confirmed they would only accept responsibility for leaves that fell directly onto the

---

9 *Daily Mail* 5th December 2006

pavement and road and stayed there. This meant that those leaves that fell onto the drive (or blew from the drive into the road) must be put in green garden waste sacks and taken to the council tip, not swept into the road with the council's leaves even though they had all fallen from the same tree and it was impossible to identify which leaves had been blown from one place to the other.

A helpful and understanding Torbay Council spokesman had the final word: 'Householders have a responsibility to deal with leaves on their property no matter where those leaves come from.'

## No Littering in the Bins

In 2007, 84-year-old retired journalist John Richards was fined because he was seen putting rubbish in… a litter bin that was attached to a lamp post.

A council sleuth used an envelope that he'd put in the bin to track him down to his address. The rest of the rubbish was kitchen scraps, which he didn't want to leave in his outside bin because the council had decided to collect rubbish only once a fortnight. He was worried about the rubbish attracting flies or even mice or rats to his tiny back yard.

Officials at Lincolnshire Council issued a £75 fine for fly-tipping, almost three quarters of his weekly pension. He was warned that if the case went to court he could be liable to pay up to £2,500. Mr Richards said: 'I just can't believe this has happened... The council should be out there on the streets, picking up litter from the pavements and roads, not snooping in bins... it would be intolerable to keep rotting food waste indoors for a fortnight until the next collection rolls around.' [10]

The council eventually withdrew the fine on the basis that 'kitchen scraps' could just as easily apply to things like apple cores and orange peel. Both

10  *Daily Mail* 16th October 2007

constitute food waste that members of the public are allowed to put into public litter bins.

Ironically, Mr Richards was handed the fine just a few days before Lincolnshire County Council launched a campaign to get people to use public litter bins more.

## Pirate Rules

In the imagination of one seven-year-old boy from Lincolnshire his garden is a pirate ship fit to rival *Pirates of the Caribbean*. The young boy, who suffers from Asperger's syndrome, even added a Jolly Roger pirate flag to complete the fantasy.

However, the household received a letter from their local council saying that the flag breached their policy on 'advertising'. An unnamed neighbour had objected to the flag and complained. The boy's parents were ordered to remove it or risk being taken to court. In response, they argued that it was ridiculous to suggest

that the flag – essentially a child's toy – amounted to advertising but they were left with no option but to make their son take it down.

They were concerned about the effect this would have on their son who finds it difficult to cope with change because of his Asperger's. His father regularly used to fly the St George's flag in his garden without attracting any complaints but let his son change it to the Jolly Roger because he loved pirates so much. However, the letter from the planning enforcement department insisted it was an offence to display 'an advert' without planning consent and condemned the 'flag pole' (fishing rod) for being higher than the allowed two metres. The family were told to remove it within 28 days or face court proceedings which could land them with a further fine of £2,500. They were offered the option of paying £95 to apply for permission to keep the flag but were warned that it was unlikely that the permission would be granted.

The council took refuge in the 2007 Town and Country Planning Act, which states that only national flags and some others, including those of the European Union and the United Nations, may be flown without permission. A spokesperson for the council said that they had 'no choice' but to act because of the law. With the relentless logic of a born bureacrat, they added: 'It might all seem a bit trivial but once it has been brought to our attention we have to ensure the law is upheld.'

The story gained mass media attention and even reached the national television news. The council finally relented and sent the family a letter of apology promising to take further action. They wrote that: 'When we receive a planning related complaint, the council has a duty to write to make those concerned aware, but accept on this occasion our letter was over the top.'

A clear case of pirate rules over jobsworth fools.

## Job Hunting Jobsworths

A job hunter, who put up flyers on lampposts around his home town, asking for someone to give him a job, was fined £75 for fly posting by his local council. He was forced to pay the fine as the council wouldn't budge on their policy of fly posting. On the plus side however, the fly posting worked. The young man got a job within a few days of putting the posters up.

## Never a Litter Bug Be

A 71-year-old grandmother was given a £75 fine for littering after a strand of cotton fell off one of her gloves. Valerie George was innocently walking on the street in her home town of Brynmawr, near Ebbw Vale, South Wales when the thread fell off her glove. Unfortunately an eagle-eyed environmental council warden saw it happen and issued her with an on-the-spot fine. She immediately protested her innocence but the delighted-to-be-useful warden insisted on taking her back to the scene of the crime, picking up the thread and proudly dangling the evidence in front of her.

'I couldn't believe my eyes,' she said 'I'm just an ordinary grandmother out shopping, not a litter lout throwing rubbish around... I had caught my watch on my glove and a piece of cotton had come off and fallen to the ground... I didn't notice. If I had I would have picked it up. I told the man it was a complete accident but he said it was still litter and to take the matter up in court... It was a strand of cotton, not a cigarette butt. I can't believe they would fine a pensioner for dropping something like that'

When Mrs George challenged the fine, council officials were adamant that a crime had indeed been committed. They asserted that even if objects fell to the ground without the wearer noticing, that person was still guilty of littering. Street cleaners were employed to clean up real litter such as food packaging and small paper items but would not tolerate random bits of fabric lying around.

The issue was vigorously contested by Mrs George and her family. Weary council officials finally conceded that they would not be pursuing the fine that would have had to come out of her modest pension. A spokesperson for Brynmawr county council would concede only that 'while we are satisfied an offence was committed, it is not in line with our priority of tackling litter more associated with affecting street cleanliness.'

## Mute the Birds

Dorothy Berry was astounded to receive a letter one morning informing her that there had been a complaint against the amount of 'bird noise' coming from her back garden and that if this did not stop, she would be handed a fine and possibly a criminal record.

The letter, from the council's environmental health department, accused her of 'nuisance caused by birds singing' and informed her that the problem was caused by birdsong 'arising from your premises during the early hours...In the interests of preventing any possible disturbance to nearby residents you may wish to consider if any such noise is likely to cause offence.' Mrs Berry, 61, who is from Fulham in West London, said, 'When I saw the letter I thought someone was larking about. I have a lovely garden in which the blackbirds sing in the trees and on the aerial of the house. But I really don't see what we can do about that.'[11] The council implied that being covered in feathers did not exempt anyone from the council's policy regarding noise pollution. For once the spokesperson for Hammersmith and Fulham Council, a fully paid up member of the Royal Society for the Protection of Birds (RSPB), showed a glimpse of humour: 'We are aware that this matter has ruffled a few feathers, but we must investigate all complaints from residents however bizarre they may appear.'

---

11 *The Sun*, 10th September 2007

## No Early Birds Allowed

In Bolton, Lancashire, a young single mum was fined £265 for putting her wheelie bins outside to be emptied earlier than her local council's rules dictated. Zoe Watmough was initially given a £75 fine for taking her bins out too early but challenged the council's decision and refused to pay. She was then summoned to court where the fine was increased to £265 including costs.

Her crime had been to put the bins behind her home the evening before they were due to be collected. To try and prevent arson attacks on bins, the council demand that they not be put out any earlier than 7.30am on the day they are to be collected. One might wonder what you were supposed to do if you were not around on bin collection day, or had to leave for work earlier than that. Council policy has, as yet, not been thought out that far.

Ms Watmough said: 'I'm flabbergasted. Surely they

should be targeting the vandals…There are people committing all sorts of crimes and getting away with it, yet I have to go to court for this, it's ridiculous… If the council are so worried about vandals they should target them, not householders.'[12]

## Lost Cat

A family who put up posters asking neighbours to look out for their missing cat were issued with a £90 fine for fly posting by their local council. Despite protests from the family, whose five-year-old daughter had been left devastated by the loss of her pet, the council upheld the fine. In spite of this run of bad luck, the cat was eventually returned to the family after being found inside the garden shed of one of their neighbours.

---

12 *Daily Express* 10th June 2008

## No Help For Disabled

When the Dewsbury Collegians Amateur Operatic Society put on a production of *Fiddler on the Roof*, some elderly or disabled members of the audience were forced to climb the stairs with no help from the supervising staff when the lift was out of order. The president of the society said town hall staff cited 'health and safety' as the reason they could not help the elderly and the infirm into the theatre. She said that one of the stewards told her that he was only there to give directions and it wasn't his job to help anyone.

The local council denied the 'health and safety' accusation, claiming that stewards were directing customers to a different door that had ramp access. However, the ramp merely got them into the building. They still had to climb the stairs to get into the theatre. As if that weren't enough the only three disabled parking bays in front of the town hall were full and many people with health problems found themselves with parking tickets despite displaying their blue badges in their cars. The council denied merrily giving out parking fines to all and sundry and claimed that only people with mobility problems were inconvenienced by the stairs.

A council spokesman gave this lengthy explanation:

'A new lift, which was installed as part of the town hall refurbishment, is currently in need of repair… Throughout the show's run, all stewards were fully briefed on what to do in the absence of the lift. While there was inconvenience for some customers, we took all possible steps to keep this to a minimum'.

'Sorry' really is the hardest word, isn't it?

## Where the Wind Blows

A man was told that he could only take his own rubbish to the council tip and was not allowed to take the odd item from his neighbours if he had space. When he pointed out to the council department that he often picked up litter from outside his house (that wasn't his), and put that in the bin, he was told that this was not allowed either because litter on the street is classified as 'commercial waste' and they weren't allowed to collect it when they came to empty the bins. He was told that it was however acceptable to pick up litter if it had blown into his garden because it would then have been re-classified as 'domestic waste'.

How anyone is supposed to keep track of all this litter blowing to and fro is a mystery that no council spokesman has been able to clarify.

## Charity Churlishness

A woman in Hull left her bag of clothing for charity next to a full charity clothing bin in a supermarket car park. Unfortunately she had left some personal papers in one of the pockets of the clothing she was donating. The council summoned her to a meeting to explain herself or pay a fixed penalty fine for 'fly tipping'. When the woman pointed out that other bags had been left there and her bag was clearly intended for the charity bin, the council simply told her that she had been identified as being one of the people who had 'dumped' the bags, and that if the others could be identified they would be.

## No Noise

The parents of a four-year-old boy were threatened with a £5,000 fine because he made too much noise when playing in the garden. Young Alfie Lansdell was ordered by Hull Council to keep the noise down or risk the huge fine.

Mr and Mrs Lansdell received a letter from council killjoys in the environmental health department, warning them their son had to be quiet in the garden or they risked being fined. If he continued to be noisy after that he could be charged a further £500 per day. The letter from the council's environmental health team claimed he was a 'noise nuisance'. It declared that the complaint related to a 'child screaming/playing in garden' and asked the parents to consider the impact this had on their neighbours. It then warned them that if the council received further complaints about the noise, Alfie's behaviour could be monitored with digital recording equipment.

The letter stated that the complainant had been asked to keep a record of dates and times when Alfie's play caused a nuisance. Simon Lansdell was astounded when he opened the letter. He said: 'Alfie is a lovely little boy. He likes to play football and skittles and play in his sandpit. . . I just can't believe the council took this complaint seriously.'[13] He added that they had tried to explain the letter to Alfie but being only four years old he didn't really understand.

The couple's closest neighbours were supportive of them and said that Alfie played out just like any other little boy. His mum Pippa said: 'It's pathetic, it's the summer holidays. Kids make noise. What am I supposed to do, gag him and put him in his bedroom?'

A presumably childless council spokesman said: 'We have to investigate any noise complaints we receive and informed Mr and Mrs Lansdell a complaint had

---

13 *The Daily Mail* 30th August 2011

been received'. He refused to comment on whether or not he believed that children should be seen but not heard.

## No Hopscotch

A family in Yorkshire were fined for 'graffiti' after their children played a game that involved drawing on the pavement in front of their house. The parents were confused because the chalk disappeared with a few rain drops but the council employee who spotted the children drawing said that defacing council property (the pavement) was a crime, whatever material was used.

## We Don't Do Fences

A family in North London were dismayed when neighbours burned down their fence after having a barbecue in their back garden. The family had bought the ex-council maisonette a few years earlier and the neighbours who burned the fence down were council tenants. As part of their leasehold bill, the family paid for buildings insurance through the council who owned the freehold. The policy clearly stated that damage to fences was covered. The neighbours who had caused the damage were tenants and couldn't pay for the fence to be mended.

However, the council refused to claim for the damage even though it was included in the buildings insurance – because the council had a policy of 'not mending fences'. The saga continued for over a year as the council refused to claim on that insurance policy or to take any action which might lead them to be seen to be mending fences.

Eventually, the family threatened to withhold part of their annual service charge which included the buildings insurance. They were finally allowed to keep the money they kept back and mend the fence themselves, one and a half years after it was damaged. All this for an insurance claim that could have been sorted out in a week.

## Skipping the Queue

A man who wanted to dispose of a lot of garden waste took his green bags to the local council tip. The tip was very busy that day and there was a long queue of cars waiting to be waved forward by the tip staff. The man saw a long line of skips, all labelled 'garden waste' and asked a member of staff why those skips couldn't be used as well. The employee told him that they had to fill up the skips one by one and could only move on to the next one when the skips were full. The queue was about an hour long at this point but the staff refused to bend the rules

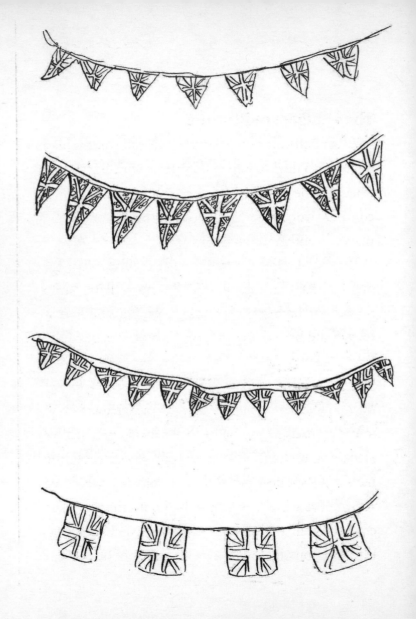

## The Dangers of Bunting

In Burnham-on-Sea, Somerset, local traders had planned to decorate the lamp posts with bunting to celebrate the Queen's Diamond Jubilee. However the council swooped in and forbade them from doing this on health and safety grounds.

The fun-loving County Council issued a statement saying that bunting couldn't be hung from lamp posts that hadn't been stress-tested to check that they could bear the weight of the plastic flags.

## Keep Off The Roof

Mr Leblond, a school caretaker in South Lanarkshire, found himself in trouble with his local council after retrieving a child's shoe from the school roof. The man was spotted by a council official, who was visiting the school, as he climbed onto the roof. The council then conducted its own 'no expense spared' investigation and found him in breach of health and safety regulations, handing him a formal written reprimand.

Parents at the school were furious at the actions of the local council jobsworths. One mum said: 'This is an example of council health and safety madness. Mr Leblond felt he had a duty of care to the school pupil and did not want him to walk home minus one of his shoes. All the parents I've spoken with are very upset at the prospect of Mr Leblond being disciplined for helping a distressed pupil in his care. The man did not want to let a little child down – it seems like a blatant case of jobsworthery.'[14]

A spokesperson for South Lanarkshire Council gave the well-worn reply: 'We do not comment on disciplinary matters.'

---

14 *The Scottish Sun* 17th May 2012

## No Bathroom? No Kitchen!

An elderly couple, renting a flat from a London council, were informed that as part of a major renovation project, the flat they rented was to be given a new kitchen and a new bathroom. The couple were overjoyed as the kitchen was in a terrible state of repair.

However, several years earlier their bathroom had been even more dilapidated. The bath was cracked and unusable and the sink was falling away from the wall. The couple wrote to the council many times explaining their dire need for a new bathroom. The only reply they ever got was that the particular block of flats they lived in was not yet due for renovation so nothing could be done. After a few years with a more or less unusable bathroom, the couple had a very basic new bathroom installed using their own savings. They thought nothing of it until employees of the firm given the renovation contract came round for an inspection. The inspector told them that because they had installed a modern bathroom, they were not eligible for a new kitchen because the contract was to replace both the bathroom and the kitchen.

The couple said that they didn't mind them replacing the bathroom as well, but the workmen told them that their contract stated that they could only replace the original bathroom, not a modern one. The couple offered to 'destroy' the bathroom themselves so it had to be replaced but the workmen were insistent that if they took the bathroom out themselves it would not be replaced.

When the couple approached the council they were given the same mindboggling explanation. Because they had put in a modern bathroom themselves, they couldn't have a new kitchen. They insisted that they had to stick to the renovation contract that had been agreed with the building company doing the renovations and the building company said they could only do what the council told them to do.

Eventually, local newspapers, radio and TV highlighted this absurd situation. Following the publicity, the couple got their new kitchen after the council drew up a new contract specifically for their property. So much money had been spent on the case that they probably could have refurbished the entire block rather than quibbling over a single kitchen renovation.

# Business Busybodies

*Until recently, it was mainly police officers, council employees and ticket inspectors who had sufficient power over us to interfere significantly in our lives. However, this role is increasingly being outsourced to shops and businesses around the country as cashiers and employees are tasked with making sure we don't have too much fun or take even the most minor of risks…*

## Blanket Ban

A woman on an overnight flight was told she couldn't use the blanket that she had brought onboard with her. She was however, allowed to buy one from the airline at the bargain price of £5.00. How long will it be before airlines work out how to charge us for the air we breathe?

## I Can't Sell You That

OK, so the government has been getting in a stew about underage drinking and threatening supermarkets with hefty fines if they sell alcohol to underage shoppers but a well-known supermarket went a step beyond the others. They raised the age limit for buying alcohol to 21 and then told staff to ask for proof of age from *anyone* buying alcohol, whatever age they were. They were told they faced paying a fine of up to £2,000 out of their own wages if they sold alcohol to anyone underage. No proof of age? No alcohol. This has resulted in some funny and frustrating scenarios for many shoppers.

An 87-year-old pensioner tried to buy a bottle of sherry at one branch but, because he'd forgotten his bus pass, he was made to go home empty-handed. He was bewildered that they couldn't just accept that he was over twenty-one.

At another branch, a woman in her sixties tried to buy two bottles of red wine. When asked for proof of her age she presented her credit card but was told that you can get a credit card when you're 18, so it isn't valid proof of being over 21. Nor, for that matter is a driving license. When the woman told the cashier that surely she must be able to see just by looking that she wasn't a teenager, she was told that it didn't matter: they had to treat every customer in the same way and needed valid written proof of age to sell alcohol to customers. The woman went home alcohol-free.

A spokesman, who enjoys condescending to alcohol drinkers, said: 'We take our responsibility with regard to selling alcohol very seriously. We do not wish to cause offence or disrespect to those persons over the age of 21. However, if a member of staff sells alcohol to an under-age customer, there is a standard fine for the individual that is set by the authorities.' He didn't confirm whether or not they were planning to completely ban anyone from buying alcohol within the next few years.

## The Dangers of Potential Smoking

A group of friends went out to the pub one Sunday afternoon and sat in the 'non-smoking' area of the garden even though two of the group were smokers. The two smokers intended to simply move to the smoking area when they wanted to smoke. One of the group went for a cigarette and came back, putting his pack of cigarettes on the table by his drink. The landlord then told the group that they had to move because they were in a 'no-smoking' area. When they all protested that no one was smoking, the landlord simply pointed to the cigarette packet and said 'but you might'. They had to move.

## How to Make Dodgems Safe

A Butlin's holiday park once banned dodgem cars from bumping into each other because of fears that holiday-makers might be injured.

## Don't Play With Scissors

A mother was banned from buying a pair of children's scissors because the shop assistant said that it was against the law.

Nadine Martin was out shopping for art supplies in West Sussex with her three-year-old daughter. She attempted to buy a brightly coloured pair of children's scissors marked 3+. Her daughter, who loved to 'help' when out shopping with mum, proudly put the scissors on the counter herself.

However, Ms Martin was astounded when she was informed that because she had allowed her daughter to hand over the scissors at the till, the store could not be certain that the child would be supervised whilst using them.

A stunned Mrs Martin said: 'She [the sales assistant] called over another woman and she said it was company policy that because she [my daughter] had put them on the counter it called into question

whether she would be supervised using them and said I wouldn't be able to buy them…I can't believe a parent can't buy plastic scissors. They were clearly labelled and had '3+' on them… It was a really innocuous little thing. When children are excited they want to put their purchase on the counter - it's a really natural thing for little ones to want to do' [15]

A spokesperson piously insisted that: 'Customer safety is of paramount importance to us. To that end we insist our staff complete regular training updates to remind them of their obligations both legally and in accordance with our own policies'. They did however reluctantly concede that the member of staff in question 'may have been a little overzealous in their interpretation of that training'.

---

15 *The Daily Telegraph* 5th March 2010

## No Pleasure at the Pleasure Beach

A ticket for Blackpool's famous fun park, the Pleasure Beach, costs around £80 for a typical family ticket, (two adults and two children). If that wasn't expensive enough, visitors to the fun fair were recently banned from taking their own picnic lunches inside, meaning they had to rely on the food for sale available inside.

An estimated six million visitors a year to Blackpool's Pleasure Beach are being told they can only eat food they have purchased on site. Staff at the entrance have been ordered to go 'sandwich searching' in people's bags to prevent them taking in any food. Many visitors have had sandwiches confiscated by 'the sandwich police' and told they can only have them back when they leave the park.

Unlike other fun parks such as Alton Towers, Thorpe Park and Legoland, the owners of Blackpool Pleasure Beach are apparently determined to limit how much pleasure can be had there. A spokesperson said: 'Due to the intensity of rides and attractions within the 42 acre site, there is limited space, and so a dedicated picnic area has been created adjacent to the entrance of Pleasure Beach. Allowances are made for guests with special dietary requirements and dedicated picnic areas are also provided for school parties booked in advance. Storage facilities are provided for those who bring outside food to the park.'[16]

---

16 *The Daily Mail* 6th May 2011

—∞—

# Banks That like
# To Say No

*Seemingly unembarrassed by having precipitated a*
*global financial crisis, our marvellous banks have*
*now moved on to a new phase, and spend their*
*days dreaming up new ways to extract money*
*from our accounts, or prevent us from making a*
*useful contribution to the economy. Here are a few*
*examples of the results…*

—∞—

## Computer Says No

One frustrated bank customer was told she would have to fly from Australia to England to close her bank account. She had forgotten to do so before emigrating to be close to her daughter's family. The account had a zero balance and no outstanding charges. In spite of offering to send proof of her identity, the bank told her she would have to attend the bank in person to close the account and advised her that the only way that this could be achieved would be for her to travel back to England.

## If You're Planning On Dying, Make Sure You Cancel Those Cards First

In 2007 a well known bank issued its annual credit card service fee to a woman who had died earlier in January the same year. When this wasn't paid they issued repeated late fees and added interest onto the late fee charges. The balance on the card had been £0.00 when she died, but eventually the fees reached £300.

A member of the lady's family, to whom the post was eventually re-directed, telephoned the bank to explain that the card holder had died nearly twelve months earlier, but the bank insisted that because they had never been informed of the death, the charges were still valid because the dead woman had inconvenienced them by failing to tell them she had died.

The family member explained that the lady had no direct close relatives and her post and details of her estate had taken over ten months to be forwarded but the bank official cheerfully informed him that it made no difference because the account had not been closed. When the relative said that he was now telling them that the lady had died and that the account should be closed, the member of staff from the bank got very excited and informed him that in that case the issue would have to be passed on to the fraud division.

The reason? The bank account had been kept active

without a valid, living account holder.

Eventually the family was passed on to a more senior bank official. He informed him that since he was not in legal control of the dead lady's estate the case could not be discussed with him. After some hours of exhaustive talks, the bank official informed the relative that there was nothing they could do because the bank's system was 'not set up for death'.

## Damned If You Don't

In 2007, at the height of the credit bubble, one of our major banks, evidently dissatisfied with their multi-billion pound profit levels, wrote to 50,000 credit customers. They were informed that unless they used their credit cards often enough, they would be charged a £35 fee for 'low-usage'.

A spokesman for the bank declined to respond when he was challenged as to the legal basis of charging people for doing absolutely nothing.

# Permits and Permissions

*There is a certain kind of individual who, when given a little authority, can't help but find more and more ways to exercise that authority. From village policemen to ticket inspectors and from council jobsworths to zealous binmen, our towns and cities seem to be thronging with people who are just itching to make our lives more difficult…*

## OAP Fined For Walking Slowly

A pensioner was given a £65 fine because she was crossing the road too slowly. Her crime was to fail to get to the other side of the road before the pedestrian light on the crossing turned back to red. Traffic police accused her of disobeying traffic signals, and being a potential cause of road traffic accidents. Despite the

protestations of the elderly lady, the police, who on that particular day had become bored of trying to catch speeding motorists, criminals, drug dealers and fraudsters, insisted on telling her that the safest speed at which to cross the road was 'around four feet per second'.

## The Wrong Sort Of Shutters

Councillors in Bacup, Lancashire created an absurd delay in the opening of a new police base because of red tape dictating what sort of shutters could be used. Inspector Judith Finney said that although the new police site was desperately needed to counteract youth crime they weren't allowed to open the new station because the council couldn't authorise the shutters that would protect the windows. She told the local Neighbourhood Forum: 'It would need to be a secure unit but we are not allowed shutters outside. We have to abide with council rules. It would increase accessibility and would be used by police officers as a base.'[17]

Bacup residents had demanded a stronger police presence in the area because of youths intimidating shoppers and going on the rampage at night. The new police centre was to be used as a base for local officers to target youth crime in the area. The council had already sold the old police station at auction to raise cash for non-policing purposes and residents were getting desperate. Bacup Traders Association chairman David Lawrie said: 'A police presence in Bacup is vital. Since the station has moved to Waterfoot, the minority of people with violent tendencies have seen that as an opportunity.'

Rossendale Council decreed that shops cannot erect metal shutters because it would ruin the appearance of the town. One could argue that broken windows have the same effect but they clearly hadn't thought it through that far.

---

17 *The Free Press* July 12th, 2012

A council spokesperson said: 'Planning say there have been some very early discussions about what would be needed. We have advised the police what would be needed. They would need to be secure and in keeping with the area... Shutters behind glass windows with lattice security grids are among acceptable alternatives"

So, it's broken windows and graffiti for the forseeable future.

## Permission to Tidy

Samantha Hamilton and her partner Colin Freeman cleared weeds and rubbish from a patch of land just outside their home. They also removed junk such as a car suspension and old bottles and beer cans. However, they were shocked to receive a letter from Surrey County Council telling them to put things back as they had been or pay for a retrospective planning application.

Ms Hamilton said: 'When trying to drive out

of our road we could not even see what traffic was coming along [the road], because the weeds were so thick and high they obscured the view . . . When we moved in, the land [in front of the house] was so overgrown with weeds that neighbours across the road were not even aware that there was a house there.[18c] Neighbours testified that the couple had performed a much-needed clear-up operation, but the council were adamant that they had to put back the weeds and rubbish or pay for clearing it. After being passed around various council departments, they were eventually told that they needed two licenses, one for clearing the rubbish and weeds and another for cutting the hedge behind it. A council spokesperson said: 'We wrote to Ms Hamilton following a complaint from a local resident, asking her to stop cultivating the land. As the highway authority we have a duty to assert and protect the rights of the public to the use and enjoy the

18 *Get Surrey* January 12th, 2012

highway. Members of the public can apply for a licence to cultivate highways land, which is what we suggested to Ms Hamilton'. The po-faced official added, 'There is a fee for the licence to be approved and for the land to be inspected to ensure the terms of the licence are met, and there are conditions indicating what can and cannot be done on the land'.

The couple refused to return the land to its original messy state and didn't pursue the licenses, reasoning that eventually the weeds would grow back, people would throw their litter there once again and then the council would be happy.

## Sumo Wrestling Is Permitted

A man in Berkshire was told he could use his revolving helipad for sumo wrestling but not for landing a helicopter. The man built the revolving pad in his garden so that he could take off in his helicopter. However, he did so without planning permission which was applied for retrospectively. Reading Borough Council granted him permission to have the turntable in his garden, where it sits flush to the lawn and is covered in grass, but told him that he could not use it to take off from. However he was told that it could be used for dining on, table tennis, rotating to get the best of the sunshine and sumo wrestling.

A councillor said: 'I regret that if everyone on the committee supports that he can't use it for his helicopter he will have spent money and wasted it, but then again he does say the main uses are recreational sumo wrestling and dining.'[19]

## The Difference a Metre Makes

Birmingham Council refused planning permission for architects to raise a garage roof by one metre on the grounds that such a height rise would be 'detrimental to the area'. The architects wanted to raise the garage

19 *Get Reading* October 20th, 2011

roof in the process of adding a third bedroom to the home. However, the council planning department insisted that their planning rules had the area marked as a conservation area and that raising the garage roof by a metre was 'out of keeping with the character of the house'. Surrounding houses have loft conversions and extensions so the owners didn't see why there would be a problem but the council were adamant that in this case the building could not go ahead.

## Colour Code Your Bags, Or Else

One local council provided different coloured bin bags for different types of waste, black for household waste and green for garden waste. Each was collected by different council departments. The green bin bags were not very strong so one householder decided to put the waste into a stronger black bag then put that into a green bag for collection. When she got home from work on collection day, her green bags had been left on the pavement. The council workmen had put a sticker on them that said: 'You have used an unsuitable type of sack.'

When she contacted the council she was told that the garden waste collectors were not allowed to collect anything in a black sack even if the black one had been placed inside a green one.

## After Hours

Licensing officers raided a village pub in Laleham in Surrey, in the belief that they were preventing an illegal late-night gig only to discover that *4am* was the name of the band not the time that they were playing.

Kate Dillon, landlady at The Feathers, was astounded when two police officers and three council officials from Spelthorne Borough Council's licensing department stormed into her pub just after 10pm. She said: 'I was outside at the time collecting glasses…I came into the pub and said 'what on earth is this all about? They wanted to know if there was going to be music on until 4am and I was absolutely speechless for the first time in my life. I'm too old to stay up that late.'[20] The two-piece soul funk band were as astonished as the landlady. Drinkers at the pub described the initial behaviour of the police officers and council officials as 'very confrontational.' Pub local Horatio Cumerband, said: 'Is this council the most stupid in history?'

It turned out that officials, from Spelthorne Borough Council, had seen an advert for 'music from 4am' at The Feathers in the *Heathrow Villager* newspaper and excitedly plotted a sting operation, presumably dreaming of fines, license revocation and heroic praise of their crafty plans. Instead they had to go home red-faced.

---

20 *The Telegraph* 19th June 2012

—⚟—

# You Don't Exist

*Jobsworths usually limit their interference to trying to prevent us from doing whatever it is we were just about to do, or fining us for whatever it was that we just did. But in one unusual case, they went a bit further...*

—⚟—

## Sorry, But You Don't Exist

Jade Jacobs-Brook had never been abroad apart from her birth, when her British parents were on holiday in Alicante, Spain. Jade's birth was registered in Spain but because her parents returned to England without a birth certificate for her, Jade was unable to prove her identity for many years.

This meant that she wasn't legally able to get a job, a passport or a national insurance number. Unlike her friends she was unable to get Saturday jobs to save up for treats or take driving lessons. She couldn't even pick up her parcels at the local post office because she had no ID.

This ridiculous saga began after UK officials refused to accept documents issued by the hospital in Alicante where she was born. Her parents hadn't known that they were supposed to inform the British Consulate in Spain of Jade's birth. If they had, they would have been issued with a valid birth certificate. To remedy the situation they contacted every official organisation they could, from the Home Office to the Foreign Office and even Buckingham Palace, to try to secure a birth certificate for their daughter but each time they were told that they had the wrong paperwork and so couldn't register their daughter as an official resident in the UK. Her dad eventually returned to the hospital in Alicante where Jade was born but they said they had no record of her birth.

At one point the helpful British government told them that it wasn't Jade's 'right' to have a birth certificate and that they weren't obliged to help someone who didn't legally exist.

A local newspaper printed her story and the firm of lawyers Allen and Overy got involved. A senior partner began to investigate the case. He said: 'I just couldn't understand why the British Government didn't step in and work with the Spanish Government. She was left to sort out a case that no private individual would have had a chance of doing... It was impacting on her human rights.'[21]

The law firm agreed to take on the case free of charge to help Jade finally get some proof that she existed. The Spanish branch of their company eventually located documents related to Jade's birth in the Spanish hospital. The case took three years to reach a resolution by which time the lawyers finally had enough information to show the sour-faced British bureaucrats that Jade really was who she claimed to be.

After a twenty year battle through British and Spanish bureaucracy she was finally issued with a birth certificate live on air at the BBC. She told of her delight that she would finally be able to go abroad – just not to Spain.

---

21  BBC 27th March 2012

—⟩⟩⟩—

# Fighting Back

*Many stories of jobsworth behaviour end with po-faced officials insisting they acted correctly or denying responsibility. We thought that it would be nice to end with a story in which the victims of jobsworth behaviour successfully fought back and won...*

—⟩⟩⟩—

## How to Get Your Bins Emptied

In 2008, infuriated residents in Huddersfield,West Yorkshire, who had seen their household waste build up during a strike by Kirklees Council workers, formed a human barricade to stop refuse collectors leaving their street without collecting their rubbish.

When the strike had finished, the bins were emptied, but the many extra bin bags which had accumulated during the strike were left on the side of the road. Residents asked for a special collection and were told a 'rapid response' vehicle would be sent. But the rubbish was still festering two weeks later. On the normal collection day, the crew said they could not take the extra bags. Residents offered to load them on to the back of the refuse truck themselves, but the crew wouldn't let them do so.

Finally, resident Mark Copley used his car to block the lorry in. The excess bags were grudgingly taken, but the crew then attempted to leave without emptying the bins. Out of sheer frustration, Mr Copley and his neighbours then formed a human wall. After a further 15-minute stand-off, the bins were eventually emptied and the wagon left, but not before police had been called and asked to intervene to prevent 'illegal obstruction of a public highway.'

With grim inevitability, a council spokesman said the binmen had 'acted properly'. The residents were just happy that their rubbish had finally been taken away.

*Illustrations by*
**Gillian Johnson**